Split the Lark

SELECTED POEMS

R.T. Smith

Salmon poetry

Published in 1999 by
Salmon Publishing Ltd,
Cliffs of Moher, Co. Clare, Ireland
http://www.salmonpoetry.com
email: salpub@iol.ie

A catalogue record for this book is available from the British Library.

The Arts Council   Salmon Publishing gratefully acknowledges
An Chomhairle Ealaíon   the financial assistance of The Arts Council.

ISBN 1 897648 48 0 Softcover

Cover photography & design by Brenda Dermody
Set by Siobhán Hutson
Printed by Techman Ireland Ltd., Dublin

Split the Lark – and you'll find the Music –
Bulb after Bulb, in Silver rolled –

    – Emily Dickinson

Acknowledgments

Many of the poems herein previously appeared in the following volumes: *Waking Under Snow* (Cold Mountain Press, 1975), *Rural Route* (Tamarack Editions, 1981), *Beasts Did Leap* (Tamarack Editions, 1982), *From the High Dive* (Watermark Press, 1983), *Birch-Light* (Tamarack Editions, 1986), *Banish Misfortune* (Livingston University Press, 1988), *The Names of Trees* (Nightshade Press, 1991), *The Cardinal Heart* (Livingston University Press, 1991), *Hunter-Gatherer* (Livingston University Press, 1996), and *Trespasser* (Louisiana State University Press, 1996).

The author also wishes to thank the following publications in which the previously uncollected poems in this volume first appeared: *The Atlanta Review, The Atlantic Monthly, Black Warrior Review, Boulevard, The Irish Times, Irish University Review, Meridian, Poetry, Poetry Ireland Review, Verse*, and *Waterford Review*.

The author wishes to express his gratitude to the following institutions and people whose assistance, guidance and support has proved invaluable: Auburn University, Washington and Lee University, The Tyrone Guthrie Centre, the Harpers Ferry National Historical Park, Brendan Galvin, Betty Adcock, Jessie Lendennie, Reetika Vazirani, John Engels, Sarah Kennedy, John Montague, Elizabeth Wassell, and Anne Kennedy, sine qua non.

for Cindy Culpepper

Contents

1

Old Photograph (1910)	3
Widow to Her Son	4
Yonosa House	5
What Black Elk Said	6
A Victory	7
Red Anger	8
Making the Snowshoes	10
The Long Joke	11
Skull, Grim and Grinning	13
The First Days of April Bring a Stillness	14
Fearing Extinction	15
Beneath the Mound	16
Black Shawl	18

2

Prelude	21
The Names of Trees	22
This Invasion	24
Haft Blossom	25
Bear Mischief	26
Believing in a Circle	28
Concentric	29
Night Music	30
In First Light	32
Emily's Bread Cradle	34
Susan Gilbert Dickinson, 1887	35
Jubilee	36
Lullaby Angel	37
Sourwood	38

3

Split the Lark 41
Cardinal Directions 43
The Cardinal Heart 44
Audubon's Cardinal 46
Ardea Herodias 48
The Bird Carver 50
Walter Anderson's J 52
Mist Net 53
Harpwing 55
The Rushes 56
We Found 57
Vespers 58
Second Waking 59
Whittling Toward the Unseen 60
The Call 61

4

Lucia 65
Spectator 68
On Laraine's Grave Hill 70
Illumination 72
Passage to Kilronin 73
Playing the Bones 74
The Magdalene 76
Linen List 79
Full Moon with Bells 82
Lilting 84

one

Old Photograph (1910)

Everyone is brown,
a wasp nest's honeyless hue.
My grandmother stands, bashful,
with eleven other children,
her mud farmer father –
a natural tobacco stain –
and the mother in an apron.
Her own grandfather's hand
on her shoulder holds his balance.
He lost his leg in a war
where butternut colour was more
than the tint of a photograph.
Her blonde hair – white since
I can remember – is braided
to her waist. Her hands
are clasped in modesty.
Everyone blinks at the flash.
Almost no eyes can be seen.
The next year she was married.
Her wedding photo's also brown,
unfocused, torn. That was
the year she turned thirteen.

Widow to Her Son

I have taken up the dulcimer again.
I did not believe the songs would come back
from so far away, but they did.
'Old Grey Goose' was easy,
and the other joysome songs.
I remember when your pa first come courting
and we sat in the parlour
with the double dulcimer between us
and rubbed knees. The light
from a coal lamp was small,
but he was Jesus' own handsome man,
and he taught me river runs,
how to fret and feather the dark poplar
into sweet freshets of song.
He told me – knowing ma and daddy
sat in the kitchen listening close
to hear both sets of strings –
that a split quill caught
off an angel's wing makes the best pick,
and a doe's rib bone the best noter.
He was a caution, and I reckoned
we'd be married directly, and we were.
I never thought these tunes would be so easy
to find after all these years alone,
and how far away they feel,
hearing them on the one set of strings,
since my shadow couldn't catch a tune
if it had handles on it
couldn't even make the drone, but listen:
you can hear the river rising
to say a heart is not a stone.

Yonosa House

She stroked molten tones
from the heart-carved maple dulcimer
and sat like a stately sack of bones
withered within coarse skin,
rocking to corn chants, snake
songs, music of passing seasons.

Her old woman's Tuscarora hair
hung like ropes on her shoulders.
Through my young mind she wove
the myths of the race
in fevered patterns, feather colours:
sound of snow, kiss of rock,
the feel of bruised birch bark,
the call of the circling hawk.

Her knotted hands showing blue rivers
jerked nervously through cornbread frying,
pressed fern patterns on butter pats,
brewed sassafras tea in the hearth.

They buried Yonosa in a deerskin skirt,
beads and braids, but featherless.
I cut hearts in her coffin lid,
wind-slain maple like the dulcimer.
The mountain was holy enough for her.
We kept our promise and raised no stone.
She sank like a root to the Georgia clay.
No Baptist churchyard caught her bones.

I thank her hands when the maples turn,
hear her chants in the thrush's song.

What Black Elk Said

It was in the Moon When the Cherries Turn Black.
We cut birch saplings,
packed our tipis on travois
and followed the Bison Wind to the banks of the Rosebud.
But that was not a good year.
The Arapahoes we called Blue Clouds
attacked our hunting parties under the Bitten Moon,
and the leaves fled early.
In that hungry winter some say the snow reached
the ponies' withers. The elk were hard
to find, and many of our people forgot
to slit bone masks and went snowblind.
Some of the bands got lost for a while. Some died.
I think it was that winter when a medicine man
named Creeping came among us, curing
the snowblinds. He packed snow across their eyes
and sang the song from his dream.
Then he would blow on the backs of their heads
and sing *hey hey hey hey*, and they would see.

It was about the dragonfly
whose wings wear eyes that he sang,
for that was where he claimed his power lay.
We also spoke to the snow of dragonflies,
and soon the deep patches melted
and the hunters brought us fresh meat.
Creeping left one night on a pony drag.
Some say he was a man of much craziness,
and I thought so too, but the next summer
I had my vision of giants slanting down like arrows
from clouds. They sang the song of the elk
speaking with the sacred voice.
The next year was the good year.
A song was singing me.

A Victory

Certain acts survive. I recall
one rural Georgia scene:
the cottonmouth that abandoned
the Flint River bottom
to inhabit the cotton field
and sleep among dry weevils
inherited the hoe's steel
blade arcing across the sun.
Grandma clove the moccasin,
declaring under her homespun bonnet,
'There, sir. Serves you right.'
The black spade head
yawned a coffin's satin,
thrust fangs in the dirt,
shot the tongue's
impotent lightning.
The dusty muscle whipped
as she bent, then rose.
Amid arid furrows and snowball
cotton, she brandished
weapon and victim in her bare
harvest hands, straddled the row
and shouted with ador,
'Got one!' Shouted, 'Mine!'
Wasp-waisted cousins,
joyous and red-fleshed with June,
danced in the clover field.
One bull groaned at the fence.
Did the irises burst into bloom?

Red Anger

The reservation school is brown and bleak
with bugs' guts mashed against walls
and rodent pellets reeking in corners.
Years of lies fade into the black chalk board.
A thin American flag with 48 stars
hangs lank over broken desks.
The stink of stale piss haunts the halls.

Tuscarora.

His reservation home is dusty.
His mother grows puffy with disease,
her left eye infected open forever.
Outside the bedroom window
his dirty, snotty bother Roy
scratches the ground,
like the goat who gnaws the garden.

Choctaw.

His father drinks
pale moonshine whiskey
and gambles recklessly at the garage,
kicks dust between weeds in the evening
and dances a fake-feathered rain dance
for tourists and a little cash.
Even the snakes have left.
Even the sun cannot stand to watch.

Cherokee.

Their limping dog sniffs a coil of dung
near the outhouse where
his sister shot herself with a .22.
So each day he marches
two miles by meagre fields
to work in a tourist lunch stand
in their greasy aprons.
He nurses his anger like a seed,
and the whites would wonder why
he spits in their hamburgers.

Tuscarora, Choctaw, Cherokee...
the living trail of tears.

Making the Snowshoes

She sits by the lodge fire
bending hickory limbs, shaping
lithe saplings cut on the north side
for slower growth and firmness.
A Crow woman from South Dakota, she forms
two hoops and ties them tight
with hide strips she has chewed soft.
Her hair reflects lustre of a raven's flight.
The wind drifts flakes against the lodge.
She learned this skill at her mother's side.
Lacing splits of soft wood,
she weaves a loose web, thinks
of her man out hunting game, leaving
blue prints as he stumbles
over the earth's white mask.
How long ago did she leave the land
where her father slew buffalo?
How long have her hands bled with effort,
moving like wounded deer in the shadows?
Knotting the thongs, she blesses
each flat basket, waves the feathered
medicine stick and makes a small song.
Her eyes hold the colour of smoke.
Her voice keeps the gold of the fire.
The ancient strength of hickory,
speed of the wild beast whose skin
secures the withes that will spread
his weight, carry him into winter,
make the hunter of doe and stag,
the comfort of her frozen nights, float
like a holy man over the burning snow.
Her skill will bring him home.

The Long Joke

The Plains Indians had a game
in which one tribe imitated another,
mimed their dress, medicine bags,
parfleche and paint. A stranger
coming into camp might mistake
Crow for Cheyenne, Paiute for Sioux,
and never know why he had been fooled.
In the Winter of the White Buffalo
a Dakota brave entered a hunting camp
on the Lower Rosebud, convinced
he was meeting friendly Oglala.
Three days he stayed, took pemmican
and slept in one clan's lodge,
warmed his heart by their fire and tales.
When he left, gifts changed hands –
a steel-headed axe, a wampum band,
plumes from a blue bird with no name.
A year later the brave was told
he had stayed with his sworn enemy,
the nomad Arapaho. He believed he could
hear the grass laughing. In rage
he searched the Black Hills, called
on every Manitou he knew for revenge.
But the Long Joke tribe was gone,
vanished into the river, risen
into clouds or dissolved in pollen.
In dusk he tore his hair and swore
to live alone forever, so great
a fool did he feel. But what he
suffered seems to miss the point.
The false band became a legend, lost
in Canada's snow. They played the Long

Joke for fifteen years, forgot the sound
of their native tongue and dream,
became their own final victims.

And so it seems some sadness cannot die.
The Long Joke is being played by every
surviving tribe, dancing to false music,
hiding their vision in paint,
following the bird with no name.

Skull, Grim and Grinning

I forgot how barbed wire snarls –
like a low bird's nest – caught
the cold raccoon last winter.
He found his own death there,
and each snagged stage of ice,
sun and hungry birds had a say
as weeds blew and I found
human need to occupy me.
But after thaw I went walking,
saw a twisted root (spring's
first threat of a snake), red eye-
shape of new sumac leaves,
deer tracks by the hundred,
and on the rotted fence post
polished to blinding shine by sun,
the forgotten relic hung,
a barbed cocoon circling
a fanged white flower of bone.

The First Days of April Bring A Stillness

The moon falls soft
as a red feather through the trees.
Cicadas enjoy the warmth
with their chants.
In another season dry shells
will lie in the dying grass,
the cicadas gone to sheer song.
But tonight something once native
but now nearly alien
has settled across the land.
A stealth that is not wind
moves along the cedars.
Distant owls warn the wood
to silence, reminiscent of Cherokees.
A wreath of careful wolves
stalks just beyond the darkness.
Around the unseasonal fire
as we nod towards sleep,
our heavy breaths become songs
we have saved for these hours.
We tremble in the secret
that what we used to be
has come among us again,
suggesting an intimacy
with wilder creatures, one red
feather falling through the trees.

Fearing Extinction

The Anasazi potter who cindered
this stark shard's concave side
with a tribal design

must have sensed the chants turning sour,
must have known
to hide his craft inside the vessel, yet no
totem, no fetish,

no vigil in the kiva
sufficed. The whole cliff-dwelling nation
vanished forever.
                    We have the ruins,
a mound of plain
clay pots, rude glyphs in rock,
sorrow for a culture's loss
and the astronomer's promise

that *any* dying star cools
on the surface,
while within, all substance
tightens and burns.

Beneath the Mound

Deer, lightning, bluebird, toad –
someone has drawn figures
on the small walls of my chamber,
this hollow under a hill.
I can hear the thirsty roots stretching.
I can feel the damp soil settling.
I sleep uneasily and long to be whole.

Most of my weapons and masks
are dust. Most of my vessels
are broken, returned to their source.
The cloth that once wrapped me
has lost all holding power.
The river is dry and cannot be healed.
Dark stones in a pattern
are the only stars I behold.

Who remembers that night,
that fire, the weeping women
in procession, slaves hauling
earth to build this mound?
Who recalls the sacred chants?
Who can dance the steps of death?
Who knows the dialect
and stories that named my tribe?

If I could weave my spirit to memory,
memory to ligament and muscle,
I could gather these fragments.
If I could recover the taste
of the black yaupon drink or skills
that kept my hunting silent,
I could refledge this dusty flesh.
I could quench this urge to move.

Yet this famine grasps me,
a rock preventing the spring's water
from surfacing under the moon.
If I could coax this cracked jaw to move,
I could rise to summon the rain.
If I could see the sky at all,
I would catch the bluebird by his wing.
If I could speak, I could sing.

Black Shawl

Hand-me-down of soft cotton
woven no closer than a mist net
for catching birds, yet she claimed
it kept her warm, wearing it autumn
to winter in memory of a threadbare
girlhood. I remember her lifting
the folds from a drawer, face
already made for public view,
lips a fifties red, scent of My
Sin. After the lean years, after
the stockpot and meagre tea,
my colic, the dreary duplexes,
she and Father would be stepping
out for Chinese at the Ming Tree
and a dance at the Shriners' Hall.
Always – unless snow, unless
a driving rain or lingering
sun – she flung the shawl across
her shoulders, as if some secret
in the weave might protect her
from loss or relapse, flat tonic
in the gin, a glare from Father.
A mourner's cape, a widow's.
From the window I watched
her turn to wave, knotted tassels
whirling, the shawl spread
winglike. Somehow it served
as a safety net, but how could
she fall and why need saving, dear
mother, dear martyr, sweet crow
flying her colours at last?

two

Prelude

Born under buds and green
maple leaves, the fawn at first
lives scentless, its slender
imprint elusive in wind
where teeth and talon
wait to feast. Fearless,
is steps so brightly that
weeds lie undisturbed.
Weeks pass. Spikes grow.
The young one's life widens,
an awkward dance beneath
fledged trees. Through foliage
and new-sown fields it follows
the herd, learns the quick leap
and forage as forked antlers
give shape to its scent.
Brown now, it feeds on mast
in moonlight, finds ease
in sleeping through summer heat.
Then come strength, inherited
speed and the instinct
to vanish in brush before fall's
deadly breeze can begin to weave
odour and the predator's need,
when the sharp leaves
of the maple begin to bleed.

The Names of Trees

Sycamore, birch, larch – I have
always loved the names of trees,
and they alone have kept me
from self-loathing. A boy
in the Smokies, I climbed the black
locust to see what the next cove
held beyond the ridge. Blue
spruce were sparkling. Later I
perched in my chinaberry cradle
and picked clusters of withered
fruit brown as the Cherokee
elders' faces. One day wandering
deeper in Owl Valley's woods,
I discovered – amid blackjack oak,
hackberry and silver poplar – an elm
scorched and hollowed, its bee maze
vacant in a crown chamber
and no bear sign showing. Standing
now by my naked crab apples
not likely to make it through winter,
I remember the thrill of entry,
a rank scent and showers of dark
pith. From within I could see
tupelo and buckthorn budding,
the creek willows dragging their
pale branches. I saw how the trees
sleep standing. They drop dead
hands that shrivel and go back
to roots as rations. They speak
the language of light. They are
starving angels that look over us
and divert lightning. I was

taken by the feel of woodpulp,
honey stains like sap. I felt
the bark jacket, volunteer shoots
stirring, bird hymn and silence.
No more twigs were branching,
a network of dry nerves. The last
roots were writhing. I stood,
a wick in that black candle.
I knew that the stir of a blackbird
flock as they settled. I was
Saint Joseph of the Elm
or Ariel burning. Then the birds
floated their bones as one being,
a chorus singing *water elm, catclaw,
tamarack, ridge hickory.* My
shadow in that trunk clung
to my shoulders, and the tree's
history filled me, its sad shade
long across saplings, paths,
deer and fox pausing. A horned
owl answered the moon. I tasted
mulch, woodmusk and the names
of trees – green, pale, bud-yellow,
rough and healing on the tongue.

This Invasion

All the shrill needlework
of late summer cicadas
cannot stitch these cut leaves
back into the branches.
The pear tree, the dogwoods,
a few sugar maples, oaks
of different species – all
have suffered from the mass
of crazed locusts that shed
their husks and rose,
storm clouds toward the sun,
their chirr and hunger,
then settling in the greenery
to cheat us of harvest, autumn
fire, our dwindling dreams.
Satisfied, they swarmed
northward, a column of smoke,
scriptural and fevered,
a migrant catastrophe
darkening the morning sky.
Now the shredded foliage
browns underfoot, and we dust
the augered holes in bark
while the cicadas sing as if
sweet design could mend
the season's raiment rent
by invading appetite.
But the domestic insects
sew no filigree, knit no intricate
intarsia. It is a year of remnants,
tightening of the cinch,
the song no local music can drown,
no frond nor blossom can resist,
no lament can stitch to plenty.

Haft Blossom

Eased by sunlight and trough
water from dream's secrets,
I found the axe after dawn
anchored in the oak stump,
vines wilder than morning
glory twining the ironwood
helve's curve, and high
in the arch where sap slowed
and the grain pooled most
stubbornly, a blossom of no
name arose, its petals bronze
in dewflash. Between my dry
garden and a cut cord of ash
and hickory, a marvellous
flower where my left palm's
sweat had altered, wood was
sending forth shoots of light,
fragrance, blessing against
shadows, as if the voices
of angels riding sunshafts
had touched haftwood amid
the still, birdless forest
to say, 'This is the centre;
let there be no more dying.'
As I grasped the handle
and pulled skyward, I saw
the red blade dangling roots,
felt the green vines snapping,
heard the passage of song
as the blossom dissolved
in my witnessing hands.

Bear Mischief

I am told a bear
can shinny up a honey tree
in an instant, can
force a fat paw deep
into the trove in spite
of sliding bark slabs,
gravity and angry bees.
I am told it is less hunger
than a love of sugars
and the joy of victory
and the clot of amber
on fur and maw. Also,
I have heard our ursine
cousin can run faster
than a Kenyan miler or
spy the flash of fish
in a shallow river, can in fact
catch what shimmers,
not because wild things
are enchanted, pure or
deserving, but because they
share with us a sense
of mischief, awe at the dance
of bees, ecstasy over
the cold fire of trout
in the river. These things
I am told at every turn,
and when I climb a hollow
tree or bend on stones
to plunge my hand through
the sound of the river,
I believe the hour of bear

has come round at last
and rejoice at kinship,
feast on elderberries all
morning, then look about
for a place to sleep till
all my humans yearnings cease,
give way to honey, speed,
rainbow meat and a bouquet
of claws to halt my sliding
earthwards before I'm ready.
Thereby this mischief ever
enchants me. As wildwood
ecstasy, it disperses all
sense of envy. It is a pure
immersion my best dreams
suggest I may yet
learn to deserve.

Believing in a Circle

It's healthy, this circling.
I try to do it twice daily:
round the lake clockwise after breakfast,
the other way, unwinding, as the sun sets.

Last week I saw a bird's nest
forked in a sweetgum I've passed
a hundred times in the two months
since winter cut the leaves off.
I clipped the limb and brought it home,
new catkins dangling and small black cones,
a relic of the rigorous season –
expectant sexual parts of a tree
and an abandoned shelter,
a cupped palm of twigs.
I have good reason to believe
this ambulation serves me.

Yesterday the dog found an ice patch,
a near-blue agate of cold with layers
of resistance, a regular system of shoals,
littoral, thinnest eye at the centre.

This morning I saw a dead cow
foundered under the catalpa.
Flies circled her like a halo.

Concentric

First October frost, and I am obsessed
with wood – hickory, oak and maple,
one sleek trunk of apple, sweet cedar
for kindling. I fell the trees
and haul them, then saw to stove length,
split and stack them around the cabin.
I am layering in for winter.
The stove is a cast iron idol
about to become my life's centre.

Thoreau wrote of 'a strong and beautiful
bug' that slept as egg for six decades
in the wooden leg of a farmer's table.
Slowly from its 'well-seasoned tomb,'
tooled from New England apple, the worm
gnawed his way to freedom. Perhaps hatched
by heat from some clay mug of cider,
the insect, obsessed, pursued his instinct,
his chewing the first music of flight.

Nights, I adjust the air ducts, toss logs
as a form of worship. The metal ticks,
measuring the season that stalls
and measures me. Patience, patience
is the flame I learn to trust.
Soon the first birds will bring their song
and I will be free in new-blooming spring.
Meanwhile, burning my way out,
I am waiting to find my wings.

Nightmusic

Listen. One by one
the wisteria
pods beyond the window

are popping
after three nights
of frost, and the beech

leaves, fallen
at last, curl,
each in its rind

of ice. A dog
scratches the storm
door. An oak log shifts

in the stove. Alone
here, I have learned
a little: how

the season whittles
back to bone,
how to stay warm

with no other
voice to sweeten
the room, how close is

anger, how cold.
As Orion strides
across the horizon

I imagine a host
of migrant birds
breathing easily

along the stripped
willow. Soft beads
of a rosary? Brown

flowers on a vine?
Never mind. Sleepy
before the firescreen's

backlit *fleur-de-lis*,
I listen for seeds
spilling rough-husked

on the lawn.
In tune
with solitude's

calibrated tones,
sparrow by sparrow,
I count my way home.

In First Light

The post oak's new growth is
gold in first light; pollen
drifts aureate in mild wind.

On the pond the sun is cool.
Oxeye daisies now open.
Morning has evil at bay.

I stand on the dew-jewelled
shore and whip my wrist, feel
the keen flex of the cane.

Nearby honeybees seek sap
in a long-leaf pine's needles.
Their quiet song is my song.

Already one fine bream gives
his last breath in wet grass
lining my reed creel.

Already I reel again against
swift tension and envision
clean flesh bathed

in butter, swimming again
in the black skillet's circle,
the season's scent.

Then a new sound overhead:
A small blue heron takes wing,
sweetens all air under his effort,

and all spring collects as he
glides above his reflected twin
and lights on a supple limb.

Bird, fish, flower, sun and wave,
any guile only distantly alive:
all these songs are my song.

Emily's Bread Cradle

Just here she stood in the heat
and light of high summer,
the sun a gong still shimmering.
She bent at the table and poured
well water into the bluest bowl,
added fistfuls of flour and dug
her hands into the mire, as white
dust dazzled the air. Forcing
the mixture in braided fingers,
she turned to the bread cradle,
as the morning jays skirmished
under a linden she could see
through dimity sheers. One lock
of her hair dangled, a wisp
of disorder she imagined might
delight Mr. Herrick. Dough clouds
smudged her brow like a sign.
If ever she saw the curved board
as a cradle, the unmade lump a child
that could be covered with moist
linen that it might rise, she kept
quiet. Still, love was always
in her deft touch. Dust to dust,
bread upon the waters. A calm
woman sweating over daily work,
she folded butter, rosemary
and salt to preserve the loaf,
and those who broke it, those
who went forth on the long road,
who could not live by bread alone.

Susan Gilbert Dickinson, 1887

Beside the tinted parlour window
I cannot excise from my thoughts
our sister, just a year gone. Nights
by the lamp, I squint at her poems'
dark words, stitches across the snow.
Nor is frost the only turn of time
that brings her home. Quick wrens
in the orchard, a lily bent low –
all pivots of season fell within
the 'circumstances' – her word – of her
exacting soul. In Austin's eyes
and Vinnie's quiet, she glows, hardly
the ghost Amherst thought it saw.
True, she haunted the house where
she wrote, a spirit without comfort.
She thought she sinned to doubt,
but erred more to believe.
Each syllable and trope shaped her
regimen of flour and flowers, chronic
pain in her temples. The stations
of her worship were lace and shadow,
and though she strained to focus
as Bright's Disease fogged her eyes,
still she was inspired to emit
that ecstasy – I mean it literal, *out
of the body* – sadly missing in our
one tintype, though evident in her
many stanzas, a scripture of stitches,
as I said, mending snow that elects
Emily, her white habit, our loss.

Jubilee

Some nights in the summer months
sea creatures crawl up on the beach.
Old folks claim they can predict it.
Science can't tell us a thing.
On the east shore of Mobile Bay
I have seen perch, snapper and flounder
flip like jewels on the sand,
shrimp and manta ray dance
like celebrating natives,
a crab gone mad with something
in his blood he could not name
try to climb a saw palm,
as if evolution were trying to prove
itself in one crazed migration.
We all ran down to the tide's leavings,
boots on and the blue gigs flashing
tines as if to keep the ocean
from changing its mind about the gift.
We collected the bounty
and marvelled at the sharpened moon
as cook fires lit up the beach.
Soon we feasted upon the manna cast
on sand, sang the season,
danced the steps of our ancestors
and slept the sleep of men
who have touched the source of dreams.

Lullaby Angel

to Francesca

At first, a song in darkness, the hum
of a reed pipe tuned
to lure you off, and if you light
a candle, you'll see wings subtle

as camphor, a body so fine
it's nearly not there, a splinter
of starlight brushing you softly
as a lover's kiss or a fallen strand

of hair, until it starts to crawl
into your skin, and some whisper
in the air tells you not all elegance
is fair. Before you host

this flattering bangle, beware
her flashing eyes, the lull
of her touch as slight as breath.
The queen mosquito hovers,

persistent as a ghost,
and blood is what this angel's
after. Her lullaby is disaster,
her glow the blaze of anger.

The sleep she brings is death.

Sourwood

for William Matthews

When the keeper has died,
whose hands have touched
so much honey,

the village will convene
to elect a successor
and to remember

the sweetness of his voice,
the dependable hymns,
the spell of smoke

and the hush just after.
While the elders
resist the old rhythms

of grief, no one will speak
of the ancient belief –
how the beefather's demise,

kept secret, could cause
the death of the hives
in the coming winter.

Then the question will rise
in a nervous murmur:
who will tell the bees?

three

Split the Lark

Rend the song to splinters
the way it tears the air.
Trace it over meadows,
briars, spruce, the bristle

of crouching hares
until the source is clear –
a breast of softest yellow.
Then lure it to a snare,

sheer away the feathers'
delicate speckling,
the finest silk of skin.
Plunder with your fingers

the colours cloaked within
windpipe, jellies, heart
of the fallen meadowlark –
iris, ginger, veridian.

Savage as a raven's beak,
will you find the bliss
that engined into song?
What you thought the art

beyond counterfeit is gone.
Was it refined disguise
or a tithe of grace
made this bird a wonder,

perching amid oak leaves,
flourishing its skein
of honesty and laughter?
In scarlet experiment

your instrument is riven,
your palms a criminal-red
soiling morning grass.
Now, my skeptic, do you
still doubt your bird was true?

Cardinal Directions

In the body of a cardinal
who hops along the tamarack limbs,
cathedrals are collapsing. Whole
worlds are falling, exhausted
stars and dialects no one left
can translate. This crested finch,
red as the last cannas
wilting, is famished. He scavenges
in a dry season for pods,
cold grubs, any scrap to sharpen
his beak or hone his sight,

and also within me the tree
of bones is giving way
to gravity, the tree of nerves
surrendering, memory's tree
releasing its leaves, though my
eyes are still seeds looking
for fertile soil, and the one bird
heavy in my chest, the cardinal
heart, still has ambitions
to forage, to sing the litany
beyond language, and fly.

The Cardinal Heart

When the last
of the late-planted cannas
had cast their petals

into the shagbark's midden
and I thought
to see no more scarlet

till March,
a cardinal fell
from the bare pecan,

his red feathers bright
as the pantaloons
on one of Goya's

infant princes, red
as the Beatitudes
in print, and when

I slit the breast,
cutting past quills
and the strange mosaic

of life, I
reached deep under
the wicker of ribs

for an amulet,
a wet tearose
more miracle than

flight, art
history or religion,
then turned the soil,

hoping a heart might
sweeten the roots
toward winter blossoms,

red and remarkable
as a cardinal's
wing flame or

the cold and shriven
sun now dwindling
in distant pines

to cinders.

Audubon's Cardinal

The ailing artist shivers
in Vieux Carre and pulls
his Seminole jacket tighter,
then leans across to catch
an imagined flicker of eye.
The bird rendered on paper

stiffens, but he tells
himself it's not guilt
that prevents the miracle.
Swan, bittern, junco and
vulture – he's killed them
by the hundreds, but always

with one ambition, to sketch
a song in two dimensions –
insinuation's colour and line.
Audubon lifts the cup
of chicory to his lips,
then turns again. He wants
the bird alive, a stalled

forager perched curious
on a mulberry limb in autumn,
but the eye, despite his vigour,
is glass, the red wing brittle
as ice. His most expensive
brushes, pigments shipped

from Paris, his practiced
articulate eye – they miss
the blasphemy he's after.

He almost laughs to recall
the morning he perched high
on a sweetgum limb to watch

a brace feeding, the female
quick and oblivious over
a scatter of seeds, her mate's
brassy chak, the pitch
of a musket's dry cocking.
Hours he has laboured. Now

primaries litter the table.
Small blades. A convex lens
any taxidermist would envy.
The original skull yellows
on the sill, and Audubon
coughs, rises to wipe bristles

and bloody spittle on a rag,
then turns to his journal
and scratches with a goose
quill in sinuous cursive
graceful, almost, as flight:
cul de sac, this work is

madness, yet I'll try again.
Sleet spatters the pane,
as he lifts his silver
flute from a Persian shawl,
and scarlet music flows
as through a living bone,

improvisations against rigor,
cardinal cantatas till dawn.

Ardea Herodias

The appetite of this blue Heron,
wrote Audubon, is endless,
and I have seen them devour
fish of all kinds, aquatic
insects, young marsh-hens
and in captivity even scraps
of cheese and bacon rinds,
but indeed they prefer
fresh swimmers and disdain
to touch anything brought low
by another hunter, although
I have seen one abandon
his cypress nest nearby
the rice fields to contest
a Hawk's catch still animate
in the billhook. The bass
fell to the water and was
lost to both. On another
occasion I shot a male
on the St. John's River
and found in the throat
a fresh perch, its head
severed by the keen
beak. The fish, when
cooked, I found excellent,
but the flesh of an old
Heron itself is by no means
to my taste, not so good
as some epicures would
aver, yet they do devour
occasional seeds, especially
the splendid water lily,
which sweetens the sinews.

I myself should prefer
the meat of a young Eagle –
which it shames me to kill,
though I too am a carnivore –
or even that beacon of sorrow
by which prophets once swore,
the omnivorous scavenger
and sarcast of the willows,
you commonmost Crow.

The Bird Carver

All winter I perch on my bench
and draw the pocket knife
through pine, ironwood and birch.

My steel is the shape of a feather,
and from it fly merganser, heron,
mallard and gallinule, sliver by sliver.

An ash slab's texture mimes thermals,
a solstice wind swirling as primaries
emerge. A beak of heartwood knurl

extends to test weather, as fingers
trace the deft scapular lines,
sleek edges, articulation of crest, spur

and eye. I work while the cold light
nurtures my craft or until dulled
steel needs the grindstone's bite.

In the hearth, flame's plumage
rises, a thicket of frail reeds,
a nest. My eyes linger and forage.

Through the window, I watch a thin
gray woodgrain of sky, the late sun
a knot from which sap unfurls. Again

I rub my fingers, touch old scars,
the flesh nicks on my skin's whorls.
As the metal's temper whets on grit,

I listen: it whispers of wings, a throng
of nomad harlequins soaring. My blade's
rasp, inspired, imitates their song:

simplicity, the grace of the handmade,
things that return and belong.

Walter Anderson's J

For his alphabet the painter
chose this blue quarreller
and lifted him out of nature

to perch eternal over pine
and cypress, his Prussian
feathers, jet crest and fine

profiled eye angel-elegant
in the sabal palm. The print
above my hearth is irreverent

and wild. The turned bird's
beak points to the russet word
of his name, floating absurdly

in swamp foliage silkscreened
on rice paper. His sin
amid the tree's scalloped fans

is pride, framed behind glass
that holds the winter of my face
as well. His gulf-coast curse

is almost audible on nights
when Jeremiah's just flights
of bitter rhetoric ignite

me and every letter shivers
like wind in a jay's feathers.
The painter rendered him vulgar

as he is in nature, sibylline
and raucous, a washed heaven's
pure verb silent in art's prison,

ravenous, indigenous, kin.

Mist Net

As if some spider gone
scientific at twilight
has decided to snare

a herd of sparrows, I
raise my web between
hillside birches and

hope for a low moon
and scuttling in the brush
to startle the birds,

that I might hear
the wild wings thrashing
unharmed in nylon mesh,

that I might inspect
each hostage to verify
myths about size,

migration, the weight
of autumn feathers. All
science aside, I yearn

just once to caress
sleek necks, to feel
the fast hearts small

as burdock burrs against
my palm. I want to cast
them up, so many dark

stars soaring, wishbones
needling north above
the dry forest, briefly

blemished with my
human touch, secretly
burning with song.

Harpwing

In the absence of fire, a barn swallow
flew down the dark path, backtracking rumours
of smoke. Bewildered, perhaps fleeing rain,
he emerged from my hearth to fly fast
at the windows and walls, soiling the room
with birdlime and soot, wings printing
his terror like dark notes on a page.

When I entered, I caught his panic,
thinking: burglar? then: bat? I switched
on the lamp to find him corner-cowering,
his black feathers damaged by the crashing,
thin muscles trembling. I caught him then,
the frail craft hysterical but still
in my palms, wings stiff as dark harps
mute in the season of silence, of cold.

No way to test his flying, so I set him
on the porch rail and stood back to watch,
until he vanished, a blur of starved
harmony joining night's black chord,
the province of storm-washed stars.
Inside again, I lit dry tinder and saw
flame fly. Light sweetened the room.
A wild music inside of me dawned.

The Rushes

are hollow as the bones of birds,
and some nights on the marsh
when the wind is gentle but firm
as the hands of the breeder,
wing-like, entering the dovecote,
a redwing blackbird may light, back
to the wind, on a green cattail,
a poppy glowing on each shoulder
as he trembles
to the softest song rising
from the throats of a longing
that will never fly.

We Found

We found an owl by the waterhole,
dead two days, maybe three.
His feathers still picked
at every passing breeze, though
the beetles were already in his eyes.
The scent was nearly unbearable,
but also almost sweet.
The wings were stiff as in mid-flight.
The cause of his demise?
On whim we pried open the beak,
amazed so small a jaw could still
be that strong across death.
The choke pellet was intact,
a clutch of rag fur, a claw,
half a slight spine twisted.
Each shred and scrap had lost its name.

Tonight as wind feeds itself
and all things light or winged fly,
the creature we found by water
must flex a rigid hinge, recall
the feel of air rushing the eyes,
the desperate, fast sounds of dark.

In the midst of dream I rise
saying aloud my Christian name.

Vespers

A cedar waxwing gray
on the gatepost holds
a wet seed in his beak,
surveys the lawn, blue
spruce fringe shaking.
A parasite burrowing
in his wing feathers is
working, a cyst
in his belly thickens.
He drops the seed
to recite his two notes,
and the twilit yard,
chilly as it darkens,
becomes the green
church of his yearning,
the parish of his
sweetest dying need.

Second Waking

Birdflash and birdsong
the morning after storm.
I can still hear the tornado's
freight train, see its lightning
in forsythia frenzy.
Black sticks littering the lawn,
overturned trash bins,
uproot, downfall, a scatter
of ripped tin. The dream
I was first stunned from –
was it midnight's billions
of milky stars extinguished,
the surge, a broken covenant
in the firs? Or was it
dawn's cardinal motionless
in the stripped willow,
that red catch-of-breath,
that stillness with no song?

Whittling Toward the Unseen

Whittlebone and whistlerib – it is
really wood, birch or sweet balsam,
perhaps a kindling slat. No matter,
it serves, as I sit by the window
in my shirt with its smoky odour, my
bootheels propped on the pine sill.
The blade easily enters and bites,
gains force with my wrist's pivot:
lick-a-sliver, lick-a-sliver. This
concentration of breath and pulse,
eye honed to the knife, is my gesture
toward winter. Steel whispers
to shape a keen device. The treeline
fades where the west holds its last
light blade-cautious. Shavings
curl like clock springs. The drill
spirals and shivers. Now hollow
as a wren's bone, this simple
stick is dwindling toward a voice
that will uncoil to seek an equal.
From stillness and kinbone, some
creature as creekside – say quail,
say whip-poor-will – will raise
its slipknot of birdcall across
cold air to meet heartwood's
searing lyric, flame to flame.

The Call

Calling the distant owl
who is greedy with the season,
I recall grandfather's voice
becoming the voice of the owl
to mate with some wild thing
cautious on the edge of the forest.
In this time of blown red leaves,
blood turning silently in my heart,
I crouch in the fog's blue shroud,
try to find the screech owl's tones
deep in my own throat where they have
slept unfed for nearly a dozen years.
Through the cave of my hands,
the thicket of fingers meshing,
I hoot twice the old way and wait.
An answer forms on air, westward:
a time-streaked face rises,
resembles me, smiles wide and flies.
Strong wings beat the night.
It takes my breath away.

four

Lucia

My daughter is not schizophrenic,
but clairvoyant.
   – James Joyce

I imagine her frantic in the asylum,
a birdgirl with wildwood's
eyes, in thrall to voices, arson,
sudden torpor. A mad flapper,

she stands in the sepia
photo as if stillness were torture,
her cloche hat soft as leafmeal,
lips sewn tight, her scarf a flame.

Lost in the maze of her father's
words, she was 'flighty' at first,
then filled with a medium's
radiance. 'I had been dreaming

of lilies on the river
blazing when the squall caught
me,' she whispered. 'I spoke
with ghosts from the field

of asphodel.' The doctors gave her
Tolstoy and Veronal, seawater
injections and a Swiss room
tight as a coffin. She preferred

tarot, the luxury suites
at Ivres, and calligraphy, her
Celtic letters glowing red
as cinders. Vagrant as tinkers,

the family nested in Zurich, Paris,
Trieste. She tasted claret, savoured
cochineal ink pressed from insects,
and danced 'Elektra' on the Bois

clad only in her opera cloak
with a white fox collar. She loved
chocolate and cigarettes, pulled
vanishing acts, and turned up

once in a Leinster ditch, oblivious,
her thoughts on fire. 'Isis is
calling me on the wireless. Together
we chain-smoke Sweet Aftons.'

Sibylline with fever, she writhed
in the *caisole de force*. Her
half-blind father quoted Rilke –
'Every angel is terrible' –

and believed her a savant, in spite
of her private burning. Lucia
held hunger strikes like the Penal
Irish and scorched her night

clothes. 'Malocchio,' she said,
'Beware the evil eye,' or sang
a multilingual rendition
of 'You're the Cream in My Coffee,'

then kissed every man in sight.
How near was the abyss? She was
Jeanne d'Arc, Isolde, and Anna Livia
with wanderlust and russet hair.

'I am Ulysses' issue, *tutti
fiume e incendio*. Gate of ivory,
gate of horn.' She suffered a cast
eye and frequent venereal bleeding,

drank hellebore tea, and sat
for hours rouging her cheeks.
This tinted photo cannot hold her.
It invokes the smell of spent

matches and an abandoned girl's
sparrow cry. 'I am my only sister.
My retinas are singed with God's
sorrow. *Je suis toujours*

l'Irlandaise.' Lucia, Lucia, dark
phoenix still rising, wingless
uccello named for a saint of light.

Spectator

In Joyce's 'The Dead'
when the whole Epiphany party agrees
that some monks sleep in their coffins
to remind them of mortality
and do penance for our sins,

we all know the revellers are wrong,
embellishing hearsay, inviting
the grim medieval rumours into dying
Ireland, but by the time Mrs.
Malins insists that the monks are

holy men, I've already become
half Trappist, lost in the story, my
Gabriel regrets shovelled under
with Michael Furey. I'm wishing
myself south to Mount

Melleray, anticipating sanctuary,
the safety of matins and lauds,
long hours of Good Works
and Latria. I want to be free as
the pious brothers are free

of quarrelling over the wishbone,
of blowing my own horn
till the ones I love suffer and fall.
Alone with a worn book, I want
to be scourged and shriven,

to lie still in the long house
of my coffin, while outside,
snow falls softly on the crooked
crosses. But then the sweets
and sherry are served,

hostesses beaming, Gabriel
fortified for his annual address,
and I am back at the table,
a veteran spectator knowing
how false he'll ring and already

thirsty for Gretta's big scene
after 'The Lass of Aughrim.' I am
blind again to candles
in the monastic chapel. I'm deaf
to glad Latin and still,

in spite of the legendary
beauty of Joyce's story,
self-tortured beyond the snow's
tenebrous *Ego te absolvo*,
spoken softly to the world.

On Laraine's Grave Hill

I walked from Kilronan and climbed
the wall, stepped over red clover
and a hare's pelt and skeleton
to find this site where Saint Enda
raised his first church. Centuries
later, it's a ruin amid the plots
of Monica de Burca, shipwrecked
Colm MacDonagh, and Mary Flaherty,
who never outgrew her cradle.
I could record the dates of a hundred
sleepers or lie down in this
drizzle forever to contemplate
man's passing, but almost trip
into an open grave with its stone
already cut and set for Blind Sim
Mulkerren, dead this week
from a fall, who could no doubt
have taught me how to be bereft
and accept it. An angle-cut birch
slab is ready for his candle,
and as I consider the slow surrender
to worm, root and the earth's
warming weight, a shoal of birds
rises in the bay, their wingrush
saying, 'The long sleep toward
heaven comes soon enough.
You must learn to live with loss,'
as they vanish in mist. So I will
not join Michael Gill and his kin
under the primrose and maidenhair
fern, far from gull cries and a raven's
ravenous bill. I will bid Enda's

hazardous chapel farewell, collect
a fist of cowslips for poor Mary
Flaherty and scrape my boots
on the sexton's spade to step over
the dead, half stumbling in dusk,
half dancing downhill, going home.

Illumination

As if some monk bored
in the cold scriptorium
had let his quill

wander from the morning
Gospel, two tendrils
of wisteria

have scrolled
their green fervour
into the weave of a wicker

deck chair to whisper
with each spiral,
every sweet leaf

and dew sparkle,
Brother, come
with us, come home.

Passage to Kilronan

On the morning boat from Rossaveal
I listened to the outboard's knock
behind our dory creaking like coffinwood
and tugged my borrowed slicker snug
as a monk's cowl. As sea chop
and the odours of oil and salmon stunned
me, the boatman offered a flask
of brandy, saying it was a big day
for the Irish, World Cup soccer match,
the Republic against the North, but
a boy off one of the local trawlers had
been missing since dawn. I was dazzled
by sun flashing off the bow cleat
and every wavelet. I was out to study
vowels and isolation, the Gaelic
nouns not even Cromwell's henchmen
nor TV could root out. I was riding
the swell and lustre to the ruins
of a language, but the sea's pitch
and wind said grief is the only dialect
that endures. I breathed shallow
and chattered about penalties and corner
kicks as the Arans rose like loaves
in the distance. Then we struck a zone
so calm we were spellbound to silence.
On the shore where water was unsinging
itself in the old tongue, the boy's
soft body waited, wedged fast amid
the still and eloquent island stones.

Playing the Bones

Two sticks curved like ribs,
the new moon – I grip them
between proper fingers
like a heron's talon
around a trout. Still, I listen
to the sea in Sean Nations'
fiddle, surf curling cool
from Mick Tracey's flute.
When the need for a sleek
bird skirting shore fills me,
I find the quick pendulum
in my wrist and give
to music the clack and rattle
of a great blue's hinged
beak. I settle sweetly
into the rhythm, discrete,
one right thing syncopated
with the pearl sky low over
Galway Bay. While the mist
of a tin whistle rises
to show us a way back
to silence, I pantomime
something; say, a farewell
wave or wingbeats over gray
water; say, some hunger
for simple invention, a path
through whin and the wind's
whisper. I seek a passage
to melodic breath, a nest
in the waterweeds, solace
after the barman locks up.
I wind these bones warm

in their flannel cloth
and under a hint of moon
walk myself home to dream
of hollow birdbones,
stitch by stitch knitting
the most soothing tune.

The Magdalene

This gnarled stone torn
from a wall of Galway's
Magdalene Laundry

could break my table
with the weeping
that seeped into granite.

When 'wayward girls'
cast off by kin
worked for the Sisters

of Mercy, escape was
unlikely. Moth-cautious
and lonely, they laboured

with a stone of soap
to cleanse every soiled
vestment or smock. Palms

scalded, skin white as leeks,
and eyebrows bleached
threadbare, each girl tore her

knuckles on a washboard,
kept her songs secret,
and feared the pearl

virgins with their holy
uniforms and keys.
On Forster Street one

could almost hear them sobbing
and imagine the lye,
the heat and sting

of local slang – 'She's one
of the Maggies, Pour soul' –
Anna from Kinvara, Diedre

from Shule, thin Brigit
from the Maamturk
hills, all the sad

Marys. In calico shifts
they drifted wraithlike
by calor lamp or

candle, hostages
to their bodies, shorn
and weary. When the nuns

knelt at beads, the girls
crept to the kitchen
bucket for scraps, always

wary for the scrape
of a key against iron,
the clack of a keeper's

rosary. When the woman
bathed Jesus' feet
with her hair, he blessed

her, but this fist
of granite under lamplight attests
how a century

of sad ladies ate
the hard bread and ladled
broth behind a dozen

locks, craving only
one stroll by the sea
or a simple lily at mass,

and not even
an artifact grown cold
in that unholy wall can lift

a life of misery
to the song of an angel
windblown as lynched

laundry or trapped
in a scouring stone.

Linen List

Annaghmakerrig

The mulberry ink
of some matron's perfect
cursive has dried the colour
of rust, and by firelight

the ordinary words are
illuminated to scripture:
dishing cloths and common
towels, frilled pillow cases

and twilled sheets.
In the adjacent chamber
Irish girls filled the hot
press daily and whispered

about the ostler in his
livery or delicate ladies
whose oil portraits smiled
in the halls. From Cootehill

and Newbliss, Monaghan
proper and the parish called
Agabog they came, a flock
of poor girls with skin

like cream in the cat's
dish. No ballad or sketch
preserves their names
in this house called 'Rock

of the River.' Surrounded
by cows, a bog and dirty
weather, they kept every
fish napkin and doily

creased and clean
for the houseproud Powers,
who wanted each milk bottle
counted and the larder

locked. Aisling, Cliona
and half-lame Siobhan –
they lived on brown
bread, rough spuds

and filched apples.
They suffered burns
from the flatirons
and the linen mistress's

tongue. 'Mice of the house,'
she called them, and kept
every girl on the run.
Nights in their attic berths

each skivvy might ask
Blue Mary to send her
someone more dashing than
a ruddy farmer before dawn

brought the routine scolding
and treks to the kitchen.
A life of skittering about
and 'yes, mum' almost broke

them, yet spoken across
the turf stove's inferno
their whispered dreams were
less practical than cabbage –

late waking, elegant handwriting
and a jar of ink precious
as an apothecary's quicksilver,
red as the mulberry roots

rumoured to slow the blood
and ease habitual pain.

Full Moon With Bells

As the solstice moon
with its Latin landscape
rises wafer-like
above the quay,

moonlight and frost
embroider the slate
with a guidebook
Irish beauty, and I shut

off the radio's report
of your sad story –
rape by a neighbour,
the court forbidding

a foreign abortion,
the power in Rome.
Where is mercy?
The boats are in,

the city still, the priory's
new bells summoning
all of Galway to vespers.
Now I imagine you

moongazing through lace
curtains as the tides
of your body ossify,
the first blue milk

forming intricate
as snowflakes high
in the winter air.
I want to reassure you,

but the words fail me,
and neither sweet
litany nor the Host
glowing can show me

anything holy
in the bishop's decree.
The faraway moon's
ancient names I whisper–

Mare Serenitatus
and *Lacus Somniorum* –
offer no solace.
Worshippers approach

the altar, their eyes
too filled with piety
to see. In Dublin
the state ministers

caucus over blue cigar
smoke and brandy,
but no absolution
echoes in the bronze

of those vernacular
bells, as the country
ices over, *Patria
Incognita*, cold core

of the heart, dark face
of the moon.

Lilting

Donegal

In the lull just after
McKenna's reel, a girl
with a port-wine

stain upon her
throat stood delicate
as a heron, while

the hard-faced farmers
all froze. Head tilted
and both eyes closed,

she soared two octaves
and trilled as a local
grocer hummed

the drone. The surf
and bramble of Irish
syllables filled

the pub between
sill and lintel,
sweeter than linnets,

more urgent than
a crow. And the scent
of raw lavender

was anchored in it,
thrifty and radiant
as a mouse's clean

bones. Not even
the barman dared
clink a glass,

and every villager
listened, as her
wordless notes

shivered, then rose.
A century ago
on winter nights

like this, to the tune
of no instrument
but such a supple

tongue, two dozen
outlaw couples
in a shuddered

room whirled
and shuffled
to defy the priests

who banned the flutes
and smashed every
fiddle on a stone.

Within the hushed
moment before chat
and porter could

once again flow,
she held every eye
with the weary glow

of a wilting lily,
and the wind outside
was talking treason,

quiet as woodbine
embroidering a trellis
or native moss

softening the nest
of a seaside heron
who's just flown.